*With thanks to our contributing
poets who help us through their poetry
to sing to the Lord a new song:*

*"O sing to the
Lord a new song...
bless his name and
declare his glory..."*
Psalm 96

Salesian Missions wishes to extend special thanks and gratitude to our generous poet friends and to the publishers who have given us permission to reprint material included in this book. Every effort has been made to give proper acknowledgments. Any omissions or errors are deeply regretted, and the publisher, upon notification, will be pleased to make the necessary corrections in subsequent editions.

The Bridge of Faith

from the
Salesian Collection

Compiled and Edited
by Sara Tarascio

Illustrated by
Paul Scully,
Frank Massa
and
Russell Bushée

CONTENTS

Sing praise to the Lord
and proclaim all his
wondrous deeds.

Ps. 105:2

God and Myself

With the wind in my hair,
And the sun on my face,
Sure and the world
Is a beautiful place.
The fresh scent of mint
That grows by the wall,
Reminds me of faces
I often recall.

I love to awaken
Just as the dawn
Peeps over the trees,
And with my gown on,
To walk through the grass,
Still wet with the dew,
With the world all my own,
For an hour or two.

The peace and the stillness,
Left over from night,
Clings closely about me,
As dark turns to light.
My troubles are lifted,
And all that is left,
Are moments belonging
...To God and myself!

Grace E. Easley

Prayer for Today

Give me the strength,
Dear Lord, I pray,
Not for next week --
Just for today.

Let thankfulness
Replace my gloom,
My cheerful face
Light up each room.

When fear and worry
Pervade my head,
Help me refill it
With faith instead.

I pray the promise
Of each new hour
Will blossom full-blown
In loving flower!

Louise Pugh Corder

A New Beginning

In a crimson burst of glory the
    radiant dawn breaks through.
All creation is awakened, God's
    promises to renew.

The bright promise of a new day,
    for each and everyone,
Dawns anew each morning as the
    sunrise is begun.

All of the problems and the worries,
    the night has swept away...
And closed the door forever on
    the cares of yesterday.

Let us greet this new beginning
    with the dawning of the sun,
Reflecting on God's glory as
    the new day is begun.

Elizabeth B. Delea

I Thank My Lord

I thank my God, with each new day,
That He has taught me how to pray:
For beast and bird and grass and flower,
For every new and shining hour
I thank my Lord.

I thank my God at eventide
For being always by my side;
For guiding me lest I should fall,
For listening when to Him I call,
I thank my Lord.

I thank my God for everything...
Throughout my life His praise I'll sing:
I will accept His loving care,
Nor question how, or why or where
When things go wrong;

Then I will thank Him just the same
For illness, sorrow, loss or shame,
That, in affliction, I may find
New strength and faith, new peace of mind
To thank my Lord.

Alice J. Christianson

*Give thanks to the
Lord - make known
his deeds among the people.*
1 Chr. 16:8

Anticipation

The spirit in my heart awaits
The coming of the Spring
With all my senses yearning for
The beauty it will bring.

The trees will don their coats of green -
The daffodils their gold -
While other flowers with patience wait
Their colors to unfold.

The blades of grass will be a nest
For dewdrops that will fall
The birds in trees will "chitter-chatter"
Or heed each other's call.

On the horizon the sun will rise
To warm the earth below,
But only "early birds" will see
The splendor of its glow.

For those who slumber far too long
Miss nature at its best,
But I'll be up at break of dawn
To be God's morning guest.

Edna Fontaine

Dusk

It's twilight now, the pond is still
    The geese fly down the darkened hill,
The heat of day begins to ease
    In the gentle cool of evening's breeze.

My bare feet brush the dusty ground
    That marks my path without a sound,
The gypsy dog runs from my side
    To flush the grass where rabbits hide.

And God, the gypsy dog and me
    Walk on in silent reverie,
Toward the low and setting sun
    That leaves the world when day is done.

The wild bird calls the coming night
    That wakens with the firefly's light,
When dusk has settled dark and deep
    And all the world has gone to sleep.

Kate Watkins Furman

These Things He Hath Promised

The Lord did not promise
All days would be bright,
Or promise we'd never
Shed tears in the night.

For life is a mixture
Of sunshine and rain,
Of happy times, laughter,
Of sorrow and pain.

He did promise always
He'd stay by our side,
And never forsake us
Whatever betide.

He promised His grace for
Each trial and task,
His strength in our weakness - -
We have but to ask;

His tender forgiveness,
New life from above,
His peace beyond measure,
His undying love.

These things He hath promised,
These things He imparts
To all who will trust Him
With faith in their hearts.

Beverly J. Anderson

Just Like Before

When I was just a little boy
I walked with You, Dear Lord,
And talked to You - and trusted You -
And joined in Your accords
But, now, I walk alone and scared -
On roads we used to trod -
For I have lost your Guiding Hand
That kept me close to God.

Somewhere - between those days and now -
I've wandered from Your ways
And lost the faith and loving trust
That blessed my childhood days;
I've let the trials and ills of time
Destroy what used to be -
That was so great a bond of love
Between Yourself and me.

So now, I pray to know, again,
Your holy love and care
That kept me safe - in growing years -
And free of life's despair;
And I implore You hear this prayer
To take my hand in Yours
And be, again, my friend and guide -
Just like You were before.

Michael Dubina

One Day in Time

The view from my window
Is a scene to behold:
The intriguing sea
And its stories untold;
The pearly white beaches
Caressed by blue tides
That sparkle like diamonds
To dazzle my eyes;
The sea birds that frolic
And fly to and fro,
Reflecting contentment
That they've come to know;
A lighthouse that beckons
To ships gone astray;
Buoys gently bobbing
In a water ballet.
Magnificent moonbeams
Light up the night
And lend their magic
To this stunning sight.

The view from my window
I cannot contain
But its fascination
I know will remain,
For if ever I've seen
God's creative hand,
I've seen it today
Where the sea meets the sand.

Catherine Janssen Irwin

My Quiet Place

I have a very quiet place
where I can see beyond compare,
a place I know where I can dream,
I find a peace and quiet there.

I see the beauty of the sky,
And jewels in a stream that shine,
There's roses high upon a hill
Beside the place that I call mine.

Then in my very quiet place
I find my Savior there.
I tell Him all my wants and cares
As I come to Him in prayer.

And so with this -- God's love for me;
I'll keep it day by day.
For by His Grace, I want to share
With others by the way.

Pearl Jennings

*My people will live in
peace and safety and in
quiet resting places.*
Isaiah 32:18

Leaves of Gold

The trees are shedding leaves of gold
    which swirl around my feet
For the emerald days of summer
    have made their last retreat.

The crimson sunsets of July
    are now a purple haze,
And the golden days of autumn
    have set the hills ablaze.

The fields are ripe with pumpkins
    like armies on parade,
But soon they shall be eaten
    when all the pies are made.

There's frost out in the meadow
    where clover used to grow,
And the graying clouds above us
    have promised early snow.

Each season is a masterpiece
    as gently they unfold,
And my heart swells with gratitude
    each time the leaves turn gold.

Clay Harrison

God's Helping Hand

Through misfortune and through sorrow,
Through heartaches and despair,
God will sustain and comfort you
If you seek Him in prayer.

Through illness and through hardships,
Through times when you feel fear,
God will give you strength anew
And fill your heart with cheer.

Through times friends may forsake you
When you are in distress,
God's always standing by you
To bring you happiness.

When your dreams have turned to ashes
And hope seems all in vain,
Place your faith and trust in God
To help your goals attain.

When the dark of life engulfs you
And tears your heart in two,
God's helping hand is always there
To light the way for you.

Harold F. Mohn

When I Grow Tired

Sometimes when I grow tired and long to rest,
Wishing I could lay aside my load,
Feeling I have given life my best,
Smiled, so that my heartache never showed,
I am sorely tempted to complain,
Especially when blood and bone grow weak,
But then I take a longer look again,
And my lot doesn't seem so cold or bleak.

For I have memories of lovely things,
Returning to me at a moment's call.
In dead of winter there's a bird who sings,
And morning glories climbing up a wall.
I have stored securely in my heart,
The vision of a thousand summer days,
So life and I walk just a bit apart,
That I may hear the forest when it prays.

Grace E. Easley

A Sunny Day in Winter

A sunny day in winter
When the skies are cold and clear,
A respite from the dull gray clouds
That are so often here.

A sunny day in winter
When the shadows dance and play,
Awakened from their slumber
By the brightness of the day.

A sunny day in winter
And the children laugh and sing,
Delighted they can be outdoors
To run and jump and swing.

A sunny day in winter
Gives a panoramic view,
Of the mountains in the distance
With their snowcaps white and new.

A sunny day in winter
With its brightness and its cheer,
Is God's way of reminding us
That spring will soon be here.

Sue Summerton

Footprints

Footprints in the winter's snow
Crystal streamlets - winds that blow,
Frost and cold - a lonely time
Waiting for the sun to shine,
Drifts are mounting - ever high
Reaching to the blue of sky.

Footprints - little creatures dear
Leave a mark of beauty here,
As they travel - onward plod
Guided by the hand of God,
Fearless of the snow and cold
Dreaming of the sunshine gold.

Fleeting moments - quiet bliss
Wintertime is all of this,
January - tinselled time
February's valentine,
Loveliness along life's way
Footprints on a winter day.

Garnett Ann Schultz

If seeds in the black earth
can turn into such beautiful roses,
what might not the heart of man become
in its long journey toward the stars?

       Gilbert Keith Chesterton

The Rose

It is only a tiny rosebud -
A flower of God's design;
But I cannot unfold the petals
With these clumsy hands of mine.

The secret of unfolding flowers
Is not known to such as I -
The flower God opens so sweetly
In my hands would fade and die.

If I cannot unfold a rosebud
This flower of God's design,
Then how can I think I have wisdom
To unfold this life of mine?

So I'll trust in Him for His leading
Each moment of every day,
And I'll look to Him for His guidance
Each step of the pilgrim way.

For the pathway that lies before me
My Heavenly Father knows -
I'll trust Him to unfold the moments
Just as He unfolds the rose.

Man's Best Friend

I can't believe that Heaven
Wouldn't hold a space
For each precious canine
Who makes earth a better place.

I can't believe God wouldn't grant
A fair and just reward
To a dear and faithful friend
Whose worth can't be ignored.

I can't believe the time that's spent
Imparting joy and love
Would never be acknowledged
By a gracious Lord above.

Catherine Janssen Irwin

Nature Testifies

The flowers of the valley and
The lofty trees so grand
Were made by Him who lives on high
To decorate our land.

The setting sun with golden beams
Doth gild the heavens so
At eventide when work is o'er
And gentle breezes blow.

The rugged mountains touch the sky,
The broad deep oceans foam:
Each in its way tell me that God
Is still upon His throne.

Birds caroling from branches of
The trees resound the theme
That He who made the world still lives
And is fore'er supreme.

Friends, God is love. It's written on
Each spire of grass that grows;
Indelibly it's stamped upon
The petals of each rose.

Although the curse of sin has caused
The earth to bring forth thorns,
They're hidden by the blossoms that
Each day our path adorns.

All things in nature testify
That God is love and He
Desires us to be happy now
And for eternity.

Luther Elvis Albright

The Glory of God in Creation

Thou art, O God, the life and light
Of all this wondrous world we see;
Its glow by day, its smile by night,
Are but reflections caught from Thee.
Where'er we turn, Thy glories shine,
And all things fair and bright are Thine!

When day, with farewell beam, delays
Among the opening clouds of even,
And we can almost think we gaze
Through golden vistas into heaven -
Those hues that make the sun's decline
So soft, so radiant, Lord! are Thine.

When night, with wings of starry gloom,
O'ershadows all the earth and skies,
Like some dark, beauteous bird, whose plume
Is sparkling with unnumber'd eyes -
That sacred gloom, those fires divine,
So grand, so countless, Lord! are Thine.

When youthful Spring around us breathes,
Thy Spirit warms her fragrant sigh;
And every flower the Summer wreathes
Is born beneath Thy kindling eye:
Where'er we turn, Thy glories shine,
And all things fair and bright are Thine!

Thomas Moore

The Shadows
of the Evening Hours

The shadows of the evening hours
Fall from the darkening sky;
Upon the fragrance of the flowers
The dews of evening lie:
Before Thy throne, O Lord of heaven,
We kneel at close of day;
Look on Thy children from on high,
And hear us while we pray.

Slowly the rays of daylight fade:
So fade within our heart
The hopes in earthly love and joy,
That one by one depart.
Slowly the bright stars, one by one
Within the heavens shine:
Give us, O Lord, fresh hopes in heav'n,
And trust in things divine.

Let peace, O Lord, Thy peace, O God,
Upon our souls descend;
From midnight fears and perils, Thou
Our trembling hearts defend.
Give us a respite from our toil,
Calm and subdue our woes;
Through the long day we labor, Lord,
O give us now repose.

Adelaide A. Procter

Songs of Praise

In the midst of trials and testings,
When there's little we can do,
Let's just sing a song and praise God --
For His faithfulness is true.

We will find there comes a comfort,
And a calm within our soul
When we praise God for His goodness
Knowing He's in full control.

We should never save our joy songs
Just to sing when days are bright.
We must lift our praises upward
Even in the dark of night.

God is always ever listening,
Tuned to hear our songs of praise.
He will bless the heart that's thankful
And give cheer to dreary days.

Beverly J. Anderson

*The Lord is my strength. My
heart trusts in him and I find
help. My heart rejoices and
with my song I praise him.*
Ps. 28:7

We Sometimes Need to Get Away

We sometimes need to get away
    from the noise and the crowd
To find a place of solitude
    where distractions aren't allowed.

We sometimes need a hiding place
    where others will not trod,
So we can rest and meditate
    upon the things of God.

Sometimes we all grow weary
    in our struggle to survive,
But as we pause to seek His face,
    we're glad that we're alive.

A candle burned at both ends
    creates a lovely light,
But too soon the flame's extinguished -
    it will not last the night!

We sometimes need to get away
    to rest, perhaps to nod,
For then we hear the still, small voice
    which speaks the things of God.

Clay Harrison

Something About a Park

Something about a park
makes me want to live forever.
Great trees, green leaves,
and in the winter
its white world is safety
to a sparrow and to me.
I walk there feeling like a poet.
I sit there and feel love surrounding me.
There is no strife or hatred here.
Only the crisp, clean silence
of a God Who paints my dreams
into lost fairytales.
Something about a park
makes me want to live forever.

Marion Schoeberlein

Wherever I Look

Wherever I look God is present,
With beauty so rich and so rare,
The budding of trees and birds singing,
And flowers beyond all compare.

The fragrance of Springtime is drifting,
And farmers are tilling the soil,
The sun shines brightly upon us,
God's love is extended to all.

God is present when raindrops are falling,
And when snow turns the earth to pure white;
No matter what season we enter,
God is there from morning till night.

The earth and sky show His beauty,
The stars that twinkle so bright,
Wherever I look God is present,
He never is out of my sight.

Frances Culp Wolfe

31

God's Treasures

I never yearned for riches
Of silver nor of gold
The treasures I possess
Cannot be bought or sold.

God taught me how to love Him
Each day that I shall live
To give to others on my way
The best that I can give.

He holds my heart within His hands
So very tenderly
The treasures of both peace and joy
He puts inside of me.

Oh! Lord! preserve forever
These feelings deep and true
For I will be so very poor
If I stop loving You.

Edna Fontaine

*In Whom every treasure of
wisdom and knowledge is hidden.*
Col. 2:3

Priceless Treasures

There are times we get so busy
we neglect those we most love,
and a sadness fills their being
only healed by God above.

Life can pass so very quickly
and we one day realize,
had we not been so self-centered,
we'd have valued family ties.

Taking time to say I love you,
is there something I can do,
for to me you are so special,
I've just failed not telling you.

Very often all that's needed
is a sweet and simple smile,
or a hug can just do wonders,
we must go the second mile.

There are treasures took for granted,
sons and daughters, husbands, wives,
mothers, fathers, sisters, brothers,
those we loved throughout our lives.

Patience tells us, don't be angry,
wisdom says, try understand,
hope says, never quit believing,
love says, I'm the perfect plan!

There's a day when all your strivings
then will cease to be no more,
so take time while you still have it,
show love to those you adore.

Shirley McDonald

It Matters Not

Do not remind me, gentle friend,
"I shall not pass this way again,"
It matters not to me today,
Who loved each step along the way.
Thank God I have not been deprived
Of windy hills when Spring arrived,
Nor missed the Summer twilight when
The stars lit up the night again.
The sweetest moments I recall,
Were down a golden lane in Fall,
The dearest face I'll ever know,
Looked back at me through winter snow,
A heart wherein such things remain,
...Cares not to pass this way again.

Grace E. Easley

Life's Pathway

Life is just a pathway,
That leads you on and on…
The start perhaps is smooth and snug,
When love and warmth are born.
The sun sends out its radiant beams
That dance upon the trees,
The breeze displays its tenderness
And soothes your wobbling knees.
Beyond there is the cobbled road
Meandering along…
Uphill and downhill thorn and slush
Sans sunshine and sans song.
Truly it is the Master's hand
That pilots those who trust,
That face so calm and loving,
Those eyes that say "you must
keep trusting me, for I am there"
There is no room for grief -
The sun which sets in darkness
Will rise - that's firm belief.
Then why must one give in to gloom?
For Jesus stands and smiles
Stretching His hand to lead you on
Across the endless miles…

Felicia Sivagnanam

Windfall

Falling, falling from the trees
changing colors autumn leaves.
Falling, falling look and see
that they're calling you and me.

To behold the beauty of
their Creator up above.
Reddish orange and golden brown
they spiral down upon the ground.

They flutter here and flitter there
as if they didn't have a care.
They fly away into a spin
as they dance along the wind.

Up above you see them still,
glistening beyond the hills.
Falling, falling from the trees
changing colors autumn leaves.

And when the trees look stripped and bare
in the cool crisp autumn air,
remember that, at next year, too,
their beauty will come back to you.

David Fink

Simplicity and Truth

With the passing of life's seasons
And the aging of their truths,
More and more I find contentment
In the simple faiths of youth;
And I find my present yearnings
Are just honesties of life
That insure my soul's salvation
And deny me sins of strife.

I have learned - with deep conviction -
That the truest wealths of earth
Are the bonds of love and friendship
That perpetuate their worth
And the greatest of life's comforts
That fulfill me every day
Is the touch of warming graces
That endear me, when I pray.

Simple truths and honest values -
Proven ageless and divine -
That the passing of life's seasons
Have impressed upon my mind,
But it took a lot of heartaches
And the taste of many fruits
To accept these noble virtues
Of simplicity and truth.

Michael Dubina

He Touched Me...

I asked the Lord to give me strength
To face the day ahead,
For I was wandering far from home
With no place to lay my head,
And He touched me...

I asked the Lord to give me hope
For I was filled with doubt;
My heart and soul reached out to Him
As I paused to look about,
And He touched me...

I asked the Lord to give me joy,
And take away my fear;
I told Him I was sore afraid
When I felt His presence near,
And He touched me...

I asked the Lord to give me love
To share with humankind;
He smiled at me from up above,
And gave me peace of mind,
And He touched me!

Hope C. Oberhelman

The Seagull

Seagull, whence are you winging
your silent way,
High o'er the waves, borne on the wind,
tell me pray?

Are you seeking a home in
far away lands,
Miles north from this rocky shore on
Arctic sands?

Will you nest amid pebbles smooth,
round and grey,
Hidden safe in the rocks, lest the
foxes prey?

Then when days are warm and bright
will you arrive,
Once again on this coast line
to dart and dive?

Seagull, O seagull, come back to
us once more
Come back, do not stay far on that
northern shore.

Lily S. Thomas

As *birds flying*
so will the Lord of hosts
defend Jerusalem.
Isaiah 31:5

Be Thankful

There is a ladder each must climb
Until we reach the top,
Rung by rung - we make our way
We dare not look - or stop!

It's called the "Journey of our life"
Lived one-day-at-a-time
Though there be many storms and strife
We should not cry or whine.

Oh, would that we could have our say
In things both great and small,
Alas, it is not ours to will
He gives His best to all!

So, just accept whate'er life gives
Be thankful for His best!
It could be even worse you know
He'll one day give us rest!

Kathryn Wiesenhoefer

You Get What You Give

You get what you give
In like and in kind,
The trust you instill,
Is that which you find.
The joy which you spread,
Must ever return.
A lamp must be filled,
Before it can burn.

You get what you give,
In gladness or woe,
A seed must be planted,
Before it can grow.
There must be a dream,
For it to come true,
And he who would dare,
Must learn how to do.

You get what you give,
Don't ever expect
Life to lend more
Than she can collect.
All things are weighed
On the scales up above,
And he is found wanting,
...Who's empty of love!

Grace E. Easley

Footprints in the Snow

Across the carpet of the snow
I see the footprints come and go,
And some that I had seen before
I look for but I see no more,
For in the place where they had been
A white expanse has drifted in.

My life is like the fallen snow
With footprints crossing to and fro,
And some I saw but yesterday
The drifts of time have washed away,
And left in place of their impress
A drear expanse of emptiness.

Yet dear, departed friends of mine
With whom I walked once on a time,
Kept in God's care we're not apart;
I hold you close within my heart,
And there enshrined you shall not go
Like footprints in the fallen snow.

Alban Wall

The Touch Sublime

Last night you were a weed,
All battered, bent and broken,
Without a line, that I could see,
Of beauty to betoken,
But in the darkness of the night
There came a clinging snow
And now, oh battered little weed,
With beauty bright you glow.
Your limbs that looked so bent
And limp and scraggly
Are now a thing of grace and form
And lovely symmetry.
Methinks perhaps it is the same
With souls when touched with grace
And where no beauty we could see
One only needs to trace
With charities' white mantle
To show that all the time
The beauty that's within each soul
But needs the touch sublime.

Minnie Boyd Popish

. . .the whole earth is
full of His glory.

Isaiah 6:3

Gratitude

For the freshness of the April rains,
The warmth of summer's sun,
For the coolness of the evening
When the long day's work is done;
For the joy we find in music,
In art and poetry,
We offer thanks again, dear Lord,
And give our hearts to Thee.

For every dawn that brings to us
A new and brighter day,
For every proof that Thou art near
To aid us on our way;
And for each night of restful sleep
That comes to mine and me,
We offer thanks again, dear Lord,
And pledge our lives to Thee.

Michael Budenich, Jr.

Summer in the Country

The rooster crowed at sunrise
　　to rouse me out of bed
As above the cloudless skies
　　turned a watermelon red.

The smell of bacon frying
　　came creeping down the hall,
And the coffee Mom was brewing
　　beckoned to us all.

Her biscuits and her gravy
　　were made with country pride,
And while I was being lazy
　　her ham was country-fried.

Outside the smell of peaches
　　permeates the air,
And rambling roses on fences
　　are blooming everywhere.

It's summer in the country
　　where city worries cease.
As far as the eye can see,
　　man and nature are at peace.

There's honey in the beehive
　　and milk fresh from the cow...
Seems I have been blessed
　　more than Heaven should allow!

Clay Harrison

Bits of Heaven

I watched a butterfly as it
    Went thistle-stopping o'er
The meadow and I got a view
    Of beauty evermore.

I saw some seagulls on their way
    Elbowing in the breeze
And glanced a bit of Heaven there
    While resting neath the trees.

I held a kitten on my lap
    And listened to it purr;
I felt so close to Heaven that
    My heart did in me stir.

I'm thankful for the little things
    That we see day by day -
Those little bits of Heaven that
    Are strewn along our way.

Luther Elvis Albright

Contentment

The simple daily pleasures
Can make a life worthwhile -
The handclasp of a comrade,
The sunshine of a smile.

A trim, white cottage nestled
So snugly on a hill,
Its red geraniums beckoning
From every window sill.

A visit from a neighbor,
Short walk beside a child,
Snow crystals in the winter,
A summer breeze so mild.

Bees humming in the meadow,
The song of trickling stream,
A bird's nest in the orchard,
One restful hour to dream.

A quiet faith sustaining
One through all daily tasks,
Content that God has answers
Before one ever asks.

Louise Pugh Corder

Wake Me in the Morning

Wake me in the morning, Jesus -
    Let me live another day.
I have many tasks to finish;
    Many favors to repay;
Sister needs my help in painting;
    Cathy needs my help to walk
And I've, yet, to reap my harvest -
    Shuck the corn and store the stalks.

I've a thousand chores need tending -
    And a thousand more to be -
But I'll try to get them finished
    In this day You give to me.
If, however, I should founder -
    Wake me, still, another day -
For I'm really in no hurry
    To be called so far away.

I would ask that You be patient
    To command my soul Home -
Wait until I'm old and weary,
    Sad of heart and all alone;
Let me finish what needs doing
    With my heart and head and hands
And awake me, with Your blessings,
    On my life and on this land.

        Michael Dubina

Detours

I find upon the road of life
That detours make it plain
That sometimes plans laid carefully
Are lost to grief and pain.

And though I'm wont to seek escape
From detours that I see,
I know within my heart I'll choose
The detours meant for me.

I dare not take a different road,
Nor travel where I will,
For detours God alone designs
Will prove He's loving still.

Perhaps one day I'll come to know
These detours like a friend,
And cherish each and every one
That's waiting 'round the bend.

But just for now I kneel and say
A simple, fervent prayer
I'll reach the detour Death demands,
And find God waiting there.

Sister Miriam Barker, C.D.S.

The Ties That Bind The Strongest

The ties that bind the strongest,
Were never made of rope,
Free men are held together
By the sturdy hemp of hope.
The silver braid of brotherhood,
A people wear with pride,
Is not embroidered on the sleeve,
But on the heart inside.

The ties that bind the strongest,
Are of the finest thread,
Upon the spool of Faith by which
A nation gets ahead.
It takes a special kind of love,
And loyalty to make
A patriot, whose back may bend,
But spirit never break.

The ties that bind the strongest,
Are those we cannot see,
The birthright of a nation
That believes in liberty.
The hearth and home where mothers teach
Their little ones to pray,
A father's love that makes the boy
The man he is today.

The ties that bind the strongest,
Are those that fill a need,
With all a fellow faces,
He has to have a Creed.
And ours the precious heritage,
Where once the pilgrims trod,
As long as we remember we're
...One nation under God.

Grace E. Easley

The Magnitude of God

The vastness and the magnitude
 Of God astounds me so;
He's neither cheap nor stingy
 And He loves us all, I know.
Yes, everything about Him shows
 His willingness to give
In such abundance and I strive
 Each day for Him to live.

I ask you to consider for
 A moment if you will
That many flowers He created
 With the greatest skill
Are never even seen by man
 And, animals galore
Are ne'er encountered -- oh, the beauty
 That He has in store!

And no two snowflakes are alike --
 Ah, don't you see, my friend
That just a fraction of earth's beauty
 Now enhances men;
The rest is sheer abundance, yet
 It cannot be compared
To what's in store for earth's redeemed
 That Jesus has prepared.

Luther Elvis Albright

Eye has not seen,
ear has not heard,
nor has it dawned on
man what God has
prepared for those
who love Him.
1 Cor. 2:9

My Morning Walk

Thank You Lord for dew kissed mornings
    And for strength You give to me
Just to walk and see the splendor
    You created, lovingly.

Flowers blooming by the walkway
    Trees that seem to touch the sky
Lifting up my weary spirit
    Like a bird to soar so high.

Little squirrels in the treetops
    Sometimes searching on the ground
For the food that You supply them
    There they scurry all around.

As the leaves all change their colors
    To their orange or golden hues
Thank You Lord for all the splendor,
    Beauty we receive from You.

May I never cease to marvel
    Or to praise You everyday
Just to walk and talk with You, Lord,
    Gives me sunshine by the way.

Thank You Lord for all Your blessings
    May I live in such a way
That the world may see Your beauty
    Shining through me everyday.

Gertrude B. McClain

Home

Home to a robin is a cozy nest,
Eggs to keep warm, a place to rest.
Home to a woodchuck is a hole in the ground,
Tunnels for exits all around.
Home for a kitten is love and affection,
A scratch on the neck, and a cat's confection.
Home to a puppy is a master to worship,
To idolize, love, and a big bone to nip.
Home to a lion is his magnificent pride,
In Africa where, they're brought back alive.
Home to a baby is his mother's breast,
A daddy to snuggle this child richly blessed.
Home to a bee is a queen and her hive,
With hundreds of others all buzzing and live.
Home to a mother is her children and mate,
Adoring each other, and life is just great.
Home to a father is his family and joy,
His wife and children, and a new baby boy.
Home to the children is siblings around,
Mommy and daddy where love abounds.
Home to all creatures means the same,
Where families dwell, love's the game.

Ruth Moyer Gilmour

Stitch by Stitch

Life is like a pattern
With a very wide selection
Of the finest grade of fabric
For our very own creation.
There are fabrics of fine lace
Rich brocade and prize damask
If we weave with sincere interest
Then the art is a prize task.
Weave in kindness faith and courage
Trim with love and charity
In due course a pattern's forming
If you're patient you will see.
Though stitch by stitch it may seem quite lengthy
But soon the task of effort fades
When you see your brand new image
Woven in the rich brocade.

Chris Zambernard

Let's Count Your Blessings

How often do we keep wishing
    For the things we cannot secure
Instead of the graces and blessings
    That forever and ever endure.

If we really wish to be happy
    Let's put foolish wishes away;
And begin scattering seeds of kindness
    Adown our pathway today.

Let us banish each selfish motive
    Let our thoughts be clean and high
Making home a little Eden
    In the sphere we occupy.

Learning to live, living to learn
    By the strength of our Father's hand,
While treading life's thorny highway
    To the shore of the Golden land.

Until we see in the gloaming,
    The print of His wounded Feet
Faithfully following the Master
    Till the journey of life is complete.

My Home Town

The happy honeysuckles grew,
With peonies and pansies too,
Beneath a sky of deepest blue,
In my home town.

And we went skating in the cold,
And sliding down the hills, so bold;
Played "run sheep run" with young and old,
In my home town.

The mountains towering in the West,
Were filled with wild flowers, I loved best;
And leafy trees for birds to nest,
In my home town.

And folks were happier it seems,
The children laughed and dreamed more dreams,
And young men had the grandest "schemes"
In my home town.

I wonder what it's like there now,
In the old church, do heads still bow?
Do children sing, and lovers vow,
In my home town?

Dear memories of Mother sweet,
With Dad in flower garden neat,
And Sister too; I'd love to meet.
In my home town.

Jeannie Knotts

Reach For The Top

There are so many rivers we have to cross,
Before we get to the sea...
So many mountains we have to climb,
To reach the highest degree.

Not all will attain the goal that they set,
As they climb up the ladder of life,
Some dream to be rich and leaders of men,
And some to never know strife.

God didn't intend that we all be the same,
So we must be content as we are;
To each He has promised a life after death,
A life so much better by far.

We all will be equal, no peers will there be;
Free from heartaches, suffering and pain...
If we accept Jesus, who died for our sins,
Forever with God, we will reign.

Albert N. Theel

He Watches Over Me

Even on the highest mountain,
    When my soul soars high and free,
Or the valley of my teardrops,
    God is watching over me.

When the storms of life are raging,
    Like a tidal wave at sea,
Seeking peace within the tempest,
    I can feel Him watching me.

Though I walk a desert pathway,
    Parched and thirsty as can be,
Love as free as flowing rivers,
    From the throne of God I see.

When I stand before the river,
    Loneliness is all I see,
He will part the raging waters,
    As He watches over me.

When my journey here is over,
    And I cross the mystic sea,
Watching at that final crossing,
    Christ is waiting there for me.

                Gertrude B. McClain

Let Not Your Heart
Be Troubled

Let not your heart be troubled;
  you need not be afraid.
You need not fear the outcome
  before your prayers are prayed.

Tomorrow's still a mystery,
  and yesterday is gone…
Thank God for everything today,
  and know you're not alone.

Our Lord has promised comfort
  in seasons of distress,
And He will not forsake those
  who seek His holiness.

You need not fear the darkness
  for God has promised light,
So let not your heart be troubled
  throughout the darkest night.

Clay Harrison

Let not your heart be troubled;
ye believe in God, believe also in me.
John 14:1

True Faith

You must have faith within your life
In everything you do;
Faith in yourself and faith in God
Each dawning day anew.

You must believe within yourself
Each step along the way,
And faith in God that you possess
Should be your guide each day.

The pitfalls you are apt to meet
As all of us will do,
Will not be hard to overcome
If faith is part of you.

True faith will lead you through each storm
And be a beacon bright,
To make your life the more worthwhile
By keeping God in sight.

Harold F. Mohn

We Cannot Live
On Memories

We cannot live on memories
Of victories in the past.
For victories fade with time.
The glory does not last.
Each of us must have a dream
That gets us out of bed,
And drives us to an unseen goal
That ever lies ahead.
Daily we should do our best
To plan and see things through.
Not giving up, but working hard
To make our dreams come true.
Then, even if we miss the mark,
We can hold our heads up high.
We won't lose if we try and fail.
We'll lose if we don't try.

Glenda Fulton Davis

Reflections

Help me imitate, dear Lord -
Your wise and gentle ways,
    and let not yet - my voice be stilled.
I so want to sing Your praise.

I'd like to tell my friends about
the happiness I've known -
    since You came into my life,
and claimed me as Your own.

I want them to know about
the love You have to share,
    and how - if they reach out to You -
they'll always find You there.

You've helped me through some trying times,
and raised my spirits so,
    and - however long it takes -
I want them all to know.

There is no hill too steep to climb -
no journey without end,
    as long as You are waiting, Lord,
just around the bend.

Doris A. Orth

Wintertime

Wintertime shone in the valley
Wintertime danced on the hill,
Wintertime sparkled in splendor
All the world quiet and still,
Making the evergreens lovely
Snow hanging low on each bough,
Wintertime proud in its glory
Beauty untold to endow.

Wintertime smiled in the morning
Soft in the beautiful dawn,
Stealing across hill and prairie
Just when the darkness had gone,
Snow mounting high, white and glistening
So like a heavenly dream,
Everywhere, pleasant excitement
Wintertime ruling supreme.

Wintertime came to the country
Putting a chill on the air,
Precious for skating and sledding
Thrilling the little hearts there,
Wintertime, bright and enchanting
Nature - a beautiful sight,
Snowflakes met wintertime's challenge
Decking the whole world in white.

Garnett Ann Schultz

My Quiet Place

Sometimes when my heart is heavy
with the burdens of the day,
I put my thoughts together,
but find I cannot pray.
When I can't voice what I'm thinking,
and my heart begins to race
I know I can find the answers
when I go to my quiet place.

The chapel is my quiet place,
and deep peace is waiting there,
And though I cannot say a word,
God hears my silent prayer.
He looks into my heart and hears
my still unspoken word,
And when I raise my eyes to look
I know that He has heard.

The hurt I felt within my heart
no longer brings me pain,
And the visit to my quiet place
has helped me once again.
The peace within the chapel
with God's loving Presence there,
Restored my faith, my love and hope,
'cause God heard my silent prayer.

Grace A. Vollono

Heaven Awaiting

Sometimes we say
Anticipation is greater than realization -
But in Heaven
Realization is greater than anticipation.

Live wisely
You are God's Creation -
But in Heaven
You will be God's perfection.

Richard Ford

Thankful Thoughts of Praise

Thank You for the moments spent
In the arms of sweet content,
Thank You for each welcome face
And each heartfelt, warm embrace.

Thank You for a song to sing
And those gorgeous days of Spring,
Thank You for the birds on high
And each fragile butterfly.

Thank You for a hand to hold
When the world seems dark and cold,
Thank You for each night and day
That true love has come my way.

Thank You for the precious rose
And the luscious grass that grows,
Thank You for the stars and moon
And each sunny afternoon.

Thank You for Your loving care
And for always being there
When I need that trusted Friend
On Whose grace I can depend.

Catherine Janssen Irwin

O *give thanks to the* Lord
for He *is good* - His
mercy is forever.
1 *Chr.* 16:34

Little Things

It's just the little homey things,
    The unobtrusive, friendly things,
The "won't-you-let-me-help-you" things
    That make our pathway light -
And it's just the jolly, joking things,
    The "never-mind-the-trouble" things,
The "laugh-with-me, it's funny" things
    That make the world seem bright.

For all the countless famous things,
    The wondrous, record-breaking things,
Those "never-can-be-equalled" things
    That all the papers cite,
Aren't like the little human things,
    The everyday-encountered things,
The "just-because-I-like-you" things
    That make us happy quite.

So here's to all the simple things,
    The dear "all-in-a-day's-work" things,
The "smile-and-face-your-troubles" things,
    Trust God to put them right -
The "done-and-then-forgotten" things,
    The "can't-you-see-I-love-you" things,
The hearty "I-am-with-you" things
    That make life worth the fight.

Not Mine to Understand

A butterfly came fluttering by
Upon the autumn breeze;
It scaled the springtime lilac bush
And skirted past the trees.
It glided o'er the arbor, high,
All void of roses, red,
Then o'er the country garden grounds
Where flowers were put to bed.

I marvelled at the beauteous wings
Of this fall butterfly;
I wondered how it knew its course
And how it learned to glide.
But it's not mine to understand
The "how's" and all the "why's";
'Tis mine to bow in awe before
Creator God, all-wise.

Loise Pinkerton Fritz

For my thoughts are not your
thoughts, neither are your ways
my ways, saith the Lord.
Isaiah 55:8

Empty Goals

We drive ourselves for goals, in life,
Of wishfulness and whim
But seldom find content of heart
In any goal we win
For with each goal that we attain
There comes a growing need
For more and more of what we gain
Each time that we succeed;
And joys, we win, just never last -
With any single prize -
For lust is born, in rich success,
And hides within disguise -
And lust instills the heart with greed
To pamper human pride
And spurns the human ego
To be less satisfied;
So - we will strive for more and more
Each time that we succeed
Until there comes a time in life
That lights our truest need;
And, then, it is that we despair
And cast away earth's goals
To reach for God's Eternal love
And blessings on our soul.

Michael Dubina

My Green Cathedral

I have a green cathedral --
A sanctum wondrous fair --
Where I can be alone with God
And talk to Him in prayer.

My green cathedral has no pews
Except a garden seat
Around which valley lilies bloom
And waft their fragrance sweet.

With largess of the sun by day,
The moon and stars by night,
Its sky-blue ceiling has no need
For artificial light.

It has no choir except the birds,
But O, their joyful din
Impels my heart to soar and sing
In unison with them!

He wrote the carols songbirds sing
In accents wild and sweet,
And fashioned all the blooms so bright
That wave around my feet.

The great cathedrals built by man
Are wondrous fair to see,
But only God can breathe the breath
Of life into a tree.

If worldly stress shall make you seek
A private place for prayer,
Come worship God in His outdoors -
A green cathedral's there.

Gailya Godfrey

And So Together...

I saw a garden the other day,
Each flower special in its own way.
For while they bloomed each on their own,
It was together their beauty shone.

If one would need more light or air,
The others would kneel and so would share.
If one would wither for lack of rain,
The tears of the others would stem the pain.

And so together the flowers grew,
In strength and love their lifetime through.

Margie Nutter

Be kind to one another
with brotherly love
and honor.
Rom. 12:10

Renewal

Have you ever crept out early
On a lovely April day
Left the dishes on the table
And the beds in disarray...

And walked a way barefooted
While the dew was on the grass
To break the misty cobwebs
Where'er you chanced to pass?

Have you seen the lilies nodding
As they gossiped with their friends
Or caught the blackbird's colors spread
Out where the river bends?

Did you hear the robin's lilting call
As he greets the coming day
And the pine boughs whispering
Or feel the sun's warm ray?

The morning mist is lifting,
Night's dark shadows steal away
And Spring in all her splendor
Makes ready for the day.

Oh, I have chores beyond the door
A dozen more or less,
But I'll pause another moment here
Amid this loveliness.

Natalie S. Thistle

With Something Fine

I'd hate to think when life is through
    That I had lived my round of years
A useless kind, that leaves behind
    No record, in this vale of tears;
That I had wasted all my days
    By treading only selfish ways,
And that this world would be the same
    If it had never known my name.

I'd like to think that here and there,
    When I am gone, there shall remain
A happier spot that might have not
    Existed, had I toiled for gain,
That someone's cheery voice and smile
    Shall prove that I had been worthwhile;
That I had paid, with something fine,
    My debt to God - for life divine.

Hazel Bacon

A Fresh New Day

Lord...
May I start each fresh new day
    With love inside my heart,
Share each joy I feel in me
    with they who feel apart.

May I alight each soul I pass
    To grander things that be,
Heighten their existence here
    With a fonder memory.

May I bring happiness to they
    I touch along the way,
We'er it be a smile, a word -
    To brighten up their day.

If I can help one soul this day
    Even when denied
I shall feel the better for it
    Because I'll know... I tried.

James Joseph Huesgen

Tomorrow
I'll Clean the Attic

"Tomorrow I'll clean the attic," I said,
    And meant it with all my heart.
"I'll get up early with suds and broom,
    And make a wonderful start.

I'll throw away all of those useless things
    We've kept for ever so long."
So I tackled the job the very next day,
    Humming a brave little song.

But I hadn't thought of the rocking horse,
    Or the treasured, childish games,
Or the little ship carved by a faraway lad,
    Today the designer of planes.

And I hadn't thought of the catcher's mitt,
    Or the Eskimo doll that could cry!
Oh, I had forgotten what attics can do
    To a person as weak as I!

"Tomorrow I'll clean the attic," I said,
    "And everything has to go!"
Tomorrow? I'll mean it with all my heart
    In a hundred years or so.

        Alice Hansche Mortenson

Old Memories

There are those special memories
We cherish through the years,
The most of them are happy ones
A few are touched by tears.
They all become more beautiful
The older now they grow,
And with their age they take their place
As days of long ago.
They are the pictures of a past
For which we sometimes yearn,
But which we know so well is gone
And which cannot return.
They have no market value in
Our commerce of today,
They are not even anything
That we can give away.
And yet those memories can play
A most important part,
As they inspire or console
Or elsewise help the heart.

James J. Metcalfe

Dawn-Prayer

Lord, I see you in the sunrise
    And in the dew of morn,
In every star that shines above --
    In every babe that's born.

The thunder speaks to me of you,
    And every waterfall.
The babbling brook that ripples by -
    The coyote's lonely call.

I see your hand in comets grand --
    Millions of miles away.
I pray you Lord when danger dawns,
    That you will with me stay.

You filled the world with gifts to us --
    Great blessings from above.
The best that we can give to you --
    Dear God, is just our love.

        Thomas F. Halley

Hand-Me-Downs

My oldest cousin was too tall,
My youngest cousin was too small,
And that is how the family found
I was to have each hand-me-down.
When they went on a shopping spree,
Nobody ever thought of me,
For sure as anything, I'd hear,
"I have some clothes THAT child can wear!"

And so they tried it on for size,
Imagining my red-rimmed eyes
To be a sign that I was glad,
To own a dress that Clara had.
Bessie tended to be stout,
And couldn't bear her clothes let out,
So when she ordered something new,
...Guess who they gave the old ones to?

I thought at last I might have grown
Too tall to wear what Betty owned,
When Susan found that she outgrew
Her last year's coat, "still almost new!"
It was the same my first date too,
When Mary Catherine's dress of blue,
Was just my size especially when
It fit her like a second skin.

When I grow old and it is time
To leave this world, I know that I'm
Just bound to hear the Savior say,
"She can't come in here dressed that way!
I'm more than sure I have a pair
Of good used wings that she can wear."
And I'll reply in sweet accord,
"Just hand-me-down another, Lord!"

Grace E. Easley

An Autumn Twilight

The Autumn evening's filled with peace
    The night birds softly call,
A hint of frost, the waking stars
    The smoky air of Fall.

The deer pass down the wooded trail
    The years last crickets sing,
While Summer flowers bow and weep
    On fields that wait for Spring.

And I walk on in happiness
    Out where blue twilight goes,
There followed by the wolf like dog
    We call the Arctic Rose!

To see the things our God has made
    That, from the stars above
To fiery trees in Autumn's dress,
    Reflect His endless love.

Kate Watkins Furman

Because He Cares...

Although my heart be heavy laden,
And the road be hard and long,
The Lord will always walk beside me,
And will keep me from all wrong,
      Because He cares...

Although the sky be dark and dreary,
And the clouds be full of rain,
The Lord will touch me with His mercy,
And will wash away my pain,
      Because He cares...

Although my days be full of sadness,
And my nights be filled with fear,
The Lord will hold me and protect me,
And I will feel His presence near,
      Because He cares...

Although the earth be full of pitfalls,
And the mountains high and steep,
The Lord will ever lead me onward,
And sustain me in His keep,
      Because He cares!

      Hope C. Oberhelman

All This and Heaven Too

If we would try, each day we live,
To those we meet, some joy to give,
A tender word, a friendly smile -
Each act we do, to make worth while;
For God has filled us all with joy -
Each man and woman, girl and boy,
He gives us blessings rich and true -
All this and heaven too.

He smooths our pathways, dries our tears,
Tries to strengthen all our fears,
Sends us glorious birds to sing -
Gives us the Autumn, and the Spring,
Daisies with their rain-kissed faces -
Nod and curtsy, from their places,
God give us roses wet with dew -
All this and heaven too.

Marigolds were blessed by Him.
Goldenrod His heart is in,
Butterflies float here and there -
Making color everywhere.

And who can match the rare perfume,
From each peach, and orange bloom?
God gave us eyes of brown and blue -
   All this and heaven too.

Most everything was touched by Him,
   Each curly head, and dimpled chin,
Each pair of silken, lash-trimmed eyes -
Drew all their color from the skies;
Child's eyes all steeped in mystery -
   Seeing things, you cannot see;
Small baby hands clinging to you -
   All this and heaven too.

The sky so clear, the air so sweet -
The tender grass beneath our feet,
A baby's laugh, a woman's smile;
A water sparkling all the while.
The moon, the stars, the earth He gave -
Each rustling breeze, each ocean wave,
Your love for me, and mine for you -
   All this and heaven too.

Dixie Earl Bryant

Good Old Days?

How many times has someone said,
Give me the good old days,
Like Grandpa living off the land,
He had no tax to pay...

That's right, but then he also had
No switches on the wall;
He had to fill the oil lamps
Before the night would fall.

Everything he ate or wore,
He had to grow himself,
He had no store around the block,
To buy it off the shelf.

Wash the dishes, take a bath,
Or make the garden grow;
Draw water from a nearby stream,
A mile away or so...

They were good old days, for sure,
I'm glad they didn't last,
And that I'm living up-to-date,
Instead of in the past.

Albert N. Theel

The Snowbird Sings

The snowbird sings his winter song
 And sings it merrily.
When frost is sparkling in the sun
 There on the holly tree.
The lovely song of tinkling bells
 Is bright and sweet to hear,
And like the white and silent snow
 Falls softly on the ear.
So tiny snowbird sing your song
 And bless this icy dawn,
My heart beats to your melody
 Long after you are gone!

 Kate Watkins Furman

By *the breath of God*
 frost is given.
 Job 37:10

He'll Forgive

If you have lost your shepherd,
If you have gone astray,
If you're grazing in the darkness
and cannot find your way;
then take the path of righteousness
and the Shepherd you will meet,
then in another moment
you'll be right there at His feet.
He'll bed you down in pastures green
and like His sheep of old,
He'll clasp you to His bosom
and return you to your fold.

Joan Hardin

*The Lord is my
Shepherd; I shall
not want.*
Ps. 23:1

The Sheep That Stray

'Twas a sheep, not a lamb, that strayed away,
    In the parable Jesus told -
A grown-up sheep that had gone astray
    From the ninety and nine in the fold.

Out in the meadows, out in the cold,
    'Twas a sheep the good shepherd sought,
And back in the flock, safe into the fold,
    'Twas a sheep the good shepherd brought.

And why for the sheep should we earnestly long,
    And as earnestly hope and pray?
Because there is danger, if they go wrong,
    They will lead the young lambs astray.

For the lambs will follow the sheep, you know,
    Wherever the sheep may stray:
If the sheep go wrong, it will not be long
    Till the lambs are as wrong as they.

And so with the sheep we earnestly plead,
    For the sake of the lambs today:
If the lambs are lost, what a terrible cost
    Some sheep will have to pay!

A Dual Delight

Oh, the beauty of the morning
When the sun has kissed the earth,
And the blossoms in their fullness
Have sprung forth from budding birth!
It is then a vibrance grips me
And I feel newness of life,
For a glorious springtime morning
Is indeed my heart's delight.

Oh, the beauty of the evening
When the moon begins to rise,
And the moonbeams touch spring's ev'n,
Making it a paradise!
It is then I look toward heaven
Thanking God for breath of life,
For the springtime's morn and evening
Bring my heart a dual delight.

Loise Pinkerton Fritz

*For then you shall delight in
the Almighty and you shall
lift up your face to God*
Job 22:26

Bouquet of Joy

I found a new variety
Amidst my flower bed.
It wasn't golden daffodils
Nor roses soft and red.

It was a pile of silken grass
Beneath my dahlias tall.
How so much grass had gathered there
I couldn't quite recall.

I gently pushed the grass aside,
Not meaning any harm.
Then plaintiff cries did fill the air
And cause me great alarm.

I quickly put the grass in place,
Restoring all the pile,
Then tip-toed from my flower bed
And stood back with a smile.

When God looks down and sends the sun
To welcome in the dawn,
Bouquets of bunnies will emerge
And frolic on my lawn.

Toni Fulco

Wisdom

God grant me "Wisdom"
    in my soul
That I might strive
    for higher goals
Forget the "fame" that
    quickly fades
Greatest "riches" never
    stays.

Reach out to me - Your
    guiding hand
My empty heart
    may understand
"Fleeting Pleasures" no
    void can fill
The yearning for Your
    Holy Will.

A "peace" that You
    alone can give
The "Way" - The "Truth"
    The "Life" - to live
Oh, bless me now -
    while I await
One step toward heaven's
    gate to take!

        Kathryn Wiesenhoefer

The Gift

Beneath a vast and deep blue sky,
'tween waves and sand a fond goodbye;
to family gathered one last time,
before disbursed by Your design.

Not one did whisper a farewell,
yet each heart knew but would not tell;
of new bonds that will so soon bind,
and misty futures each must find.

Not just the young but elders, too,
must trod new ways to follow You.
For You have work that cannot wait.
Your guiding hand will crown our fate.

The family was Your gift to us
providing values, love and trust.
Yes, it prepared us for this time;
Lord, help us seek that we may find.

    William Marshall Weller

His Loving Arms

I walked along a country lane
And found a peaceful bower
I lingered there in solitude
Among the birds and flowers.

The sunlight filtered through the trees,
I felt its warming rays
Like loving arms enfolding me,
And brightened up my day.

No matter where the roadway leads
God's always waiting there
To welcome me with love and peace
And keep me in His care.

Dolores Karides

All Loves Excelling!

No other love can equal,
The Love of Christ our Lord;
Whom in the realms of glory,
Is worshipped and adored.

Who left His throne in Heaven,
That He might walk on earth;
To give Himself for mankind,
That all have second birth.

How can we help but love Him,
Who had so much to give?
Whom through His grace and mercy,
Didst die that all might live!

Oh precious precious Savior,
Whom now in glory reigns;
Oh may we through Thy sorrow,
Eternal rapture gain!

Sancie Earman King

A Prayer
of Thanksgiving

We thank Thee, Father, for the care
    That did not come to try us,
The burden that we did not bear,
    The trouble that passed by us.

The task we did not fail to do,
    The hurt we did not cherish,
The friend who did not prove untrue,
    The joy that did not perish.

We thank Thee for the blinding storm
    That did not loose its swelling,
And for the sudden blight of harm
    That came not nigh our dwelling.

We thank Thee for the dart unsped,
    The bitter word unspoken,
The grave unmade, the tear unshed,
    The heart-tie still unbroken.

Freedom

Freedom in Jesus is knowing the way
To trust in His plan for our lives day to day,
To discover His friendship, to grow in His Love
While singing His praises that rise high above!

Freedom in Jesus is surrendering all,
The good and the bad, the rise and the fall,
To bask in His goodness, to master His Word,
While adoring His Presence as the
"Good News" is heard!

Freedom in Jesus is having the heart
To totally give Him your life, every part,
To taste of His mercy, to believe He forgives,
While giving Him glory for Lord Jesus now lives!

For He is the answer to every prayer,
He lightens each burden, He handles each care,
He brightens dark moments, He lifts when we fall,
And He cleanses our hearts, when we heed to His call!

So each time you remember He died for your sins,
With new life in Lord Jesus, your freedom begins!

Linda-Marie Bariana

God bless you and sustain you
With each new dawning day,
God grant you grace and wisdom
To travel life's highway.

God give you strength and courage
When things perplex your mind,
God help you reach the cherished goal
You seek and strive to find.

God comfort you when in distress
And trouble comes your way,
God be with you and watch o'er you
I humbly ask and pray.

Harold F. Mohn

Remember the One

When things go wrong,
And your heart is breaking,
When dreams get shattered
That were in the making,

When tears start to fall
And the pain is too great,
When the way seems too long
and you feel you can't wait -

Remember the One
Who suffered it all,
Whose Love redeemed man,
After his fall.

He was ridiculed and mocked,
And He died just for you,
Everything you've suffered,
He has, and more, too.

He will comfort, encourage,
And calm every fear,
If you turn your heart to Him,
For He's always near.

Connie J. Kirby

I Give of Myself

Let me, O Lord, each passing day,
Give of myself along the way.
Let me extend to my fellow man,
A pleasant smile, a helping hand.
Teach me to bear the trials of life.
To help my brother in his strife.
And hopefully, when my day has run,
I'll hear the words from Thee - "Well Done."

Henry M. Goyette

When Summer Dies

There are the days when summer dies
And how they bring to me
The haunting of my yesterdays
And O... the memories.

There starts a quickening of the eve's
The early dew of days
That fall upon life's mantle
Through a certain kind of haze.

And O... how sweet it seems to me
This aura of before
'Tis when dear moments come to rest
And lay there at your door.

I feel a part of all the world
And it is part of me...
The haunting of a summer's end...
How sweet it comes to be.

James Joseph Huesgen

The Lighthouse
and the Sea

The lighthouse here
    beside the sea
    is magic-- Yes!
    it says to me,

"Come here and hear
my tales of glory!
of ocean wild,
this is my story:

    Ancient rime
    and windswept shore
    were long ago
    and evermore

of perfect rhyme
for all of time--
They give great peace
to all mankind."

    Nancy Neff Dostie

How Many Times...

How many times do we think that the road
Is too rocky for us to tread?
How many times do we long for the paths
That are flowery and smooth instead?

How many times till we understand
That the load He gives us is light
If it's shouldered with faith that He knows the way,
And that morning will dawn out of night?

How many times do we have to learn
That He's there every step of the way,
And that He will guide us, and all that He asks
Is just that we trust Him and pray?

How many times as we stumble and fall
On the way in our upward climb
Does He reach down and lift us in patience and love?
Time... after time... after time.

Lee Simmons

Winter Wealth

There's a breathlessness about winter
When the earth sparkles so,
The aspens, oaks, and maples,
Softly creak as brisk winds blow.

The ice-capped mountains whisper
And their echoes chant bold
That winter has arrived at last
With heavenly treasures to unfold.

A graceful ballet of snowflakes
Soon form a blanket of white,
These wee intricate patterns
Pirouette while swift in flight.

Enchanted by this wonderland
Children's eyes are set aglow,
With the aid of fur-lined mittens -
Snowballs grow and grow!

Sleds are flowing o'er the hills
Like restless waterfalls,
Curious woodland creatures romp
Where stately pines stand tall.

Winter's wealth glitters,
But is quick to melt away -
God bedecked it with gaiety and beauty
So grasp it while ye may!

Linda C. Grazulis

Between the Fall and Spring

The autumn leaves have faded now
The trees are dead and bare,
And tiny snowflakes, soft and white
Now sparkle everywhere,
The flowers asleep within their beds
The birds have flown away,
And all of nature is at rest
This cold December day.

It's fireside weather - happy hours
That families spend together,
A friendly chat - a time to read
Despite the wintry weather,
As early darkness now descends
The evenings can be fun,
To spend with those you love the best
When daily chores are done.

The wind more sharp - a crystal cold
Ice pictures on each pane,
So little warmth in sun of gold
A lonely world again,
A magic time of miracles
When winter reigns supreme,
A quiet fills each dreaming heart
Between the fall and spring.

Garnett Ann Schultz

103

'Tis a Little Journey

'Tis a little journey this we walk;
Hardly time for murmurs - time for talk.
Yet we learn to quarrel and to hate;
Afterward regret it when too late.

Now and then 'tis sunshine - sometimes dark
Sometimes care and sorrow leave their mark.
Yet we walk the pathway side by side;
Where so many others lived and died.

We can see the moral, understand;
Yet we walk not always hand in hand.
Why must there be hatred, greed and strife?
We do not need such shadows here in life.

Shining Hour

Tell me again of days gone by,
Help me recall the sounds and songs,
What matter if we can't return,
Back to the place where the heart belongs!
Waste not your sighs on years grown old,
Weep not for faces of the past,
Speak not again of long lost dreams,
And sands of time that flow too fast!
Within the power of all men,
The vision of a shining hour,
In every memory there clings,
The sweetness of a faded flower!
And what the heart has loved the most,
Can never be mislaid or lost!

Grace E. Easley

The flowers appear on the earth;
the time of the singing of birds is come.

Song 2:12

Country Treasures

Sunrise in the country is a lovely sight
for it's summertime, and everything is bright.
The morning glory and rambling rose
delight my eyes and tickle my nose.
Pansies, petunias and sweet peas too,
just took a bath in the morning dew.
Lilacs and zinnias and bright marigold
sweeten the air as their petals unfold.
The meadow's alive with the buzzin' of bees,
and a choir of bluebirds sings in the trees.
Red hollyhocks are growing so tall
beside the sunflowers by the old mill wall.
A hummingbird's come to visit awhile...
just watching him fly brings me a smile.
The fragrance of peach is suddenly there
on butterfly wings much lighter than air.
Each day is a treasure, a sight to behold,
and moments like these are better than gold.

Clay Harrison

Home

Home is the spot in this whole wide world
Where we trod at the long day's end,
Where we find a smile and a joy worthwhile
That a love so true can lend.

Home is the place where our hearts can rest
At the close of a weary day,
Where our hopes mount high and life's cares go by
Where we live and laugh and play.

Home is the world of the folks we love
Where peace and joy abide,
Where a child so small is our world and all
Where we build life's dreams with pride.

Home is just home in a million ways
A mother's soft caress,
A spot alone, that we call our own
And it's all that is fine and best.

Garnett Ann Schultz

Where There is Love

Where there is love the heart is light,
Where there is love the day is bright,
Where there is love there is a song
To help when things are going wrong...
Where there is love there is a smile
To make all things seem more worthwhile,
Where there is love there's quiet peace,
A tranquil place where turmoils cease...
Love changes darkness into light
And makes the heart take "wingless flight,"
And Mothers have a special way
Of filling homes with love each day...
And when the home is filled with love
You'll always find God spoken of,
And when a family "prays together,"
That family also "stays together"...
And once again a Mother's touch
Can mold and shape and do so much
To make this world a better place
For every color, creed and race -
For when man walks with God again,
There shall be peace on earth for men.

Helen Steiner Rice

Used with permission of
The Helen Steiner Rice Foundation
Cincinnati, OH 45202

Gentle Father of Your Sheep

Gentle Father of Your sheep,
Now I lay me down to sleep;
Long and hard has been the day
For this very bit of clay.
In the way temptations stood,
Mounted like a stack of wood;
Storm clouds hovered overhead,
Yet, through it all my soul you kept.

Now You've drawn the shades of night,
Still with me You will abide.
All the day You walked with me,
All the night so shall it be.
Waking, sleeping, You are there,
Keeping me within Your care;
So, Gentle Father of Your sheep,
Now I lay me down to sleep.

Loise Pinkerton Fritz

*I will lay down in peace
and sleep, for you will
keep me safe, O Lord.*
Ps. 4:8

What Is A Friend?

A friend is someone tried and true,
That you can tell your troubles to,
A gentle smile, a happy face,
That makes the world a better place.
A friend is someone that is yours,
As long as time and life endures,
Sharing cherished moments when
You know you never need pretend.

A friend is someone fair and square,
Who comforts just by being there,
A fellow traveler who brings
New meaning to the little things.
Who always has the time to say
A word to brighten up your day,
Who helps you to accomplish more
Than you have ever done before.

Who senses what you never say,
And somehow likes you just the way
You are, in spite of all you lack,
And each of us on looking back,
Recalls a voice, a special face,
No other person can replace,
Who brushes back the doubt and care,
Just because he's always there.

Because they are of such a kind,
A friend like this is hard to find,
I think by now we all have seen
That they are few and far between.
But heaven's emissary, he
Who leads us toward eternity,
Becoming a reflection of
God's deep and everlasting love.

Grace E. Easley

Please Walk With Me

If my footsteps tend to wander
from the righteous path I roam -
    Lord, please walk with me and guide me
to the road that leads back home.

    Then please let me feel your presence
throughout every passing day,
    and though at times I may be tempted -
help me just to walk Your way.

    Never let me get so busy,
so involved in selfish needs,
    that I can't find time for others -
time for good and thoughtful deeds.

    And when my life on earth is over
let my friends remember me -
    not for little acts of kindness,
but for having walked with Thee!

Doris A. Orth

Tomorrow I'll Think About God

Not today when I am so busy,
Not today when there's so much to do,
Not today while I'm young and eager
And life is far-reaching and new-
But tomorrow when I am older
And the tempo of life is less,
I'll have more time for praying
And for meditation, I guess…
But time is swift in its passing
And before we are really aware
We find ourselves growing older
And daily in need of God's care…
And while God is always ready
To help us and lead us along,
Because we have tarried and wasted
Our young days in "dancing and song,"
We find we are not well-acquainted
With the wonderful love of the Lord
And we feel very strange in His presence
And unworthy of Our Father's reward-
For only the children who seek Him
With hearts yet untouched and still clean
Can ever experience His greatness
And know what His love can mean . . .
So waste not the hours of "life's morning,"
Get acquainted with God when you're born,
And when you come to "life's evening,"
It will shine like "the glory of morn"!

Helen Steiner Rice

Used with permission of
The Helen Steiner Rice Foundation
Cincinnati, OH 45202

Cup of Tea

Come, my dear, and sit with me.
Let us have a cup of tea.
Come, my dear, I'll fill the cup.
See the white steam curling up,
The magic brew from small, curled leaf
Assuaging weariness and grief.
Or, could it be it's not the brew -
But sharing things, just we two,
That seems to wash the care away
And give fresh zest to heart and day?

Minnie Boyd Popish

My Wish for You

I wish for you a "Trust" so true
That shines through everything you do.

A "Faith" so strong it carries you
Along life's path through darkness too!

A "Steadiness" as you proceed
In times of plenty or times of need.

And may you know God's "Constant Love"
Showered on you from above.

We all share dreams - we all have hopes
Sometimes they disappear like smoke.

Our life is like an empty loom
An unknown pattern in the womb.

Its shape takes place - day by day
In everything we do and say.

We need His help - He takes our hand
And leads us through the shifting sand.

With caring heart and much love too
God's own "Peace" I wish for you.

                    Rosemary DiTaranto

Renewed

I'm a little bit older
Than I was yesterday;
My walk a bit slower,
My hair's turning gray.

I put in more effort
Just to rise out of bed,
And before I stop talking,
I forget what I have said.

The cold winds of winter
Chill me right to the bone,
Such a trek to my mailbox -
Fifty feet from my home.

But there is one thing
That gets better each day,
My relationship with God
In our talks as I pray.

Soon He will call me
To His golden shore,
I'll shuck this old body,
I won't need it anymore.

Albert N. Theel

Times of Prayer

O' joyful times of holy care
Are moments that I spend in prayer,
When only God can see me pray
And hear the quiet words I say.
These are my times of saving Grace -
When I am in the Lord's embrace
And He attends my scars of life
That are the wounds of trials and strife.

These are my havens of relief
From broken dreams and ills of grief
And from my heartaches of despair
That I - alone - could never bear.
They are my very sacred times
That God divines with peace of mind
And fills with joy and holy care:
These times I spend with Him, in prayer.

Michael Dubina

I Shall Not Grow Old

If night and loneliness disrupt my peace,
I think of all the glories of the day;
When chilling winter winds are loath to cease,
I still remember warmth and flowering May.
If I accept each challenge with a will
And laugh with youth and lend a child my hand,
I will not stop to think of every ill
While trying other lives to understand.
If I have loved my friends for their true worth
In trying times and when their fortunes shone,
There could not be a greater joy on earth
Than friendship ties to cherish as my own.
For youth is fleeting as a moth's white wings,
But age finds daily joy in simple things.

Josephine Stone Breeding

Some Say There Are No Miracles

Some say there are no miracles-
     things happen just by chance;
But who hangs the stars in space,
     and makes the moonbeams dance?

Who planted seeds when earth was born
     so we could smell the rose;
Who planted trees upon the hills
     and every bush that grows?

Who sends us rain in summertime
     and soft December snow?
Who guides migrating swallows home
     and makes the rivers flow?

Who causes tides to ebb and flow,
     the sun to rise and set?
Who gives us precious memories
     we never shall forget?

Some say there are no miracles
     upon this earthly sod,
But I have faith in things above
     which lead the heart to God.

       Clay Harrison

The Greatest Gift

I have seen God's work at sunrise
Watched the new day a-coming;
The surge of hope and wonder
Set my heart and soul a-humming.

I have listened to the music
Of His gentle birds a-singing;
It filled my heart with gladness,
Like butterflies a-winging.

I have walked amid His fields,
The amber grains a-blowing,
And felt the thrill of nature
Throughout my veins a-flowing.

I have watched His golden sunset
At day's end a-gleaming;
And felt the inner calmness
That set my mind a-dreaming.

But now I've seen my child's smile --
So enraptured there a-gazing,
And felt God's greatest gift of all --
The fire of Love a-blazing!

Sandra M. Haight

Make Room

Make room within your heart and home
For God to enter in
And know the blessings He rewards
For worship unto Him;
He will be host to all your joys
And Saviour to despair
If you make room - in heart and home -
For Him to enter, there.

No day or night will ever pass
Without His touch of Grace -
And yours will be a life of loves
That Christian hearts embrace -
For He will shepherd you - and share -
In all that life akins,
If you just open up your doors
And let Him enter in.

Michael Dubina

About Autumn

I love to see Fall coming
The sun is lower in the sky
When God is painting pictures
And the last cicadas cry.

Fall to me is many things
When all my memories rise
And flow on chilly breezes
Beneath the painted skies.

Of all the lovely seasons -
Autumn will always be
When God is so much closer
When the spirit is more free.

James Joseph Huesgen

The Golden Leaf

A golden leaf hung on a tree,
It hung on so tenaciously.
Though strong winds blew with mighty force,
It seemed to hold on all the more.
The other leaves had lost their hold
And dropped to earth...not this leaf, gold.
Though back and forth it swayed and swayed,
Still on that tree the gold leaf stayed.

Might we be like that leaf of gold;
Though strong winds blow, may we still hold
Unto our faith, our strong belief
That Christ is God; Messiah, He,
Who came to earth from heav'n above
Because God all the world so loved.
May we cling, like that golden leaf,
To Christ, our Lord, Whom we've believed.

Loise Pinkerton Fritz

Luke 18:8

Autumn Glory

Orange pumpkins in the cellar,
Red apples in the bin.
The birds are winging southward,
And snow will soon begin.

The trees have been embellished
In gowns of brilliant hue,
And just around the corner,
Cold Winter is in view.

The final blaze of glory
Which signals Fall's decline
Is God's bright Autumn message --
A vivid, wondrous sign.

Though Winter strip earth barren,
And nature seem forlorn,
The frozen earth will flourish,
In Spring will be reborn.

Louise Pugh Corder

His Pattern of Love

Our Lord laid out a pattern
Oh, how He wanted me to see
The pattern set to follow
His pattern of love just for me.

My mind once so heavily burdened
Oh, such - a - mystery!
What does my Lord; my God above
Really have in store for me?

Hours which I had spent asking
Endless questions of "why's"
The answers He set down before me
Gently placed them; and opened my eyes.

Why do I let myself question so?
The answers are always so near
When I turn to my Lord; my Savior
Every need that I pray, He will hear.

I laid all of my burdens upon Him
Right into His most Sacred hands
For I know and trust that He only
Holds the key to whatever is planned.

Our Lord laid out a pattern
"Oh yes Lord," I do see
The pattern set to follow
Your pattern of love just for me!

Carolyn T. Mokan

125

That Makes
A House A Home

It isn't curtains starched and fine
Nor windows shining clean,
Expensive paintings on the walls
That catch the sunlight's gleam,
Nor furniture so new and grand
The many things you own,
For not a single one of these
Can make a house a home.

It matters not a speck of dust
To real folks this won't count,
Nor that you have the worldly things
In any large amount,
A house can never be a home
However hard you'd try,
Unless the welcome's friendly there -
A twinkle in your eye.

It takes a handshake firm and true
A greeting warm and gay,
An air of love and happiness
As we would go our way,
'Tis these that make a house a home
Though worldly things are few,
And folks will always come again
But just because of you.

A house can never be a home
However long we live,
Unless it's filled with friendliness
With laughter we can give,
Whatever else we chance to have
How much we gain or own,
'Tis only people real and true
That make a house a home.

Garnett Ann Schultz

Faith looks across the storm -
    It does not doubt
Or stop to look at clouds
    And things without.

Faith does not question why
    When all His ways
Are hard to understand,
    But trusts and prays.

It seeks the greatest gift
    And asks not sight;
It does not need to see -
    He is its light.

Above the tempest's roar
    It hears His voice;
And, with its hands in His,
    Faith can rejoice.

It fears no cloud, or wind
    That it can bring;
Faith looks across the storm
    And still can sing.